THE TRANSCONTINENTAL RAILROAD IN UTAH

— KATHY KIRKPATRICK —

For my children, who are able to enjoy the cultural diversity in Utah today

America Through Time is an imprint of Fonthill Media LLC
www.through-time.com
office@through-time.com

Published by Arcadia Publishing by arrangement with Fonthill Media LLC
For all general information, please contact Arcadia Publishing:
Telephone: 843-853-2070
Fax: 843-853-0044
E-mail: sales@arcadiapublishing.com
For customer service and orders:
Toll-Free 1-888-313-2665

www.arcadiapublishing.com

First published 2019

Copyright © Kathy Kirkpatrick 2019

ISBN 978-1-63499-134-6

All rights reserved. No part of this publication may be reproduced, stored in a retrieval system or transmitted in any form or by any means, electronic, mechanical, photocopying, recording or otherwise, without prior permission in writing from Fonthill Media LLC

Typeset in 10pt on 13pt Sabon
Printed and bound in England

CONTENTS

List of Illustrations   5
Introduction   7

1. History   9
2. Religious Groups   13
3. Building the RR   21
4. The Transcontinental Railroad Route Through Utah   23
5. Protestants   77
6. Ethnic Groups   83

Appendix: Museums and Websites   91
Bibliography   92
Acknowledgments   94
Index   95

LIST OF ILLUSTRATIONS

Map of Bidwell–Bartleson Party	10
Map of Bureau of Land Management Transcontinental Back Country Byway	10
Echo Canyon Pony Express	11
Weber Pony Express Marker	12
Ogden Third Ward, 1856, WSU	14
Iosepa Cemetery	14
Promontory Main Street	15
Auerbach Store in Corinne	16
1870 Corinne	17
1870 Ogden	18
General Connor monument	20
Sacred Heart	20
Telegraph	22
Construction at Chemin de Fer	24
Trestle at Dale Creek	24
Citadel Rock and Bridge	25
Main Street, Bear River City	25
Mezzanine	26
Railroad workers	26
Union Pacific Construction train	27
1,000 Mile Tree	27
Map of Stops: Wyoming to Promontory	28
Echo Canyon	28
Wahsatch, 1870	29
Wahsatch today	29
Castle Rock today	31
Emory	31
Echo Iron Rails Sign	32
Echo history	32
Echo station	32
Croydon	33
Morgan station	33
Peterson Cemetery	34
Uintah, 1870	34
Uintah, today	34
First railroad station at Ogden	35
First trains at Ogden station	35
Ogden, 1876	36
Ogden station, today	36
Willard cemetery	38
Brigham city station	38
Construction at Bear River	39
Corinne opera house	39
"The Burg on the Bear" poster	40
"Corinne in its Hey Day" poster	40
Promontory map	41
Trestle at Promontory	42
Big Fill	42
Blasting a tunnel	43
Building a trestle	43
American River	44
Chinese crews working	44
Repair crews working	45
Coaling on the road at Wannemacker	45
Railroad workers with tools	46
Snow galleries	46
Truckee depot	47

Grading, Hart	47	Champaign	69
Chinese RR Workers Camp	48	Directors of the railroad companies	69
Chinese track-laying crew	48	Broad view of the last rail	69
Map of stops: Nevada to Promontory	49	Workers laying the last rail	70
Bureau of Land Management Transcontinental Back Country Byway at Promontory	49	The paymaster	70
		Union and Central Pacific Railroad ad	71
Lucin Bureau of Land Management Transcontinental Back Country Byway	49	Competition 1869	71
		Curved trestle, Secrettown	72
Lucin Bureau of Land Management marker	51	"Cuts and Fills"	72
Around Lucin with Bureau of Land Management marker at center	51	"A Grand Anvil Chorus"	73
		"Rungs of a Ladder"	73
Lucin Cut-Off map	52	"Tunnels and Trestles"	73
Watercress	52	Union Pacific opening ad	73
Near Watercress	53	Leslie cartoon (1)	74
Between Watercress and Terrace	53	Leslie cartoon (2)	74
Bureau of Land Management sign from HWY 30	54	Chinese marker, Promontory	75
		Irish marker, Promontory	75
Terrace, Utah	54	UPRR at Ogden	76
Terrace marker	55	1883 map	76
Ombey marker	56	St. Mark, Salt Lake City	78
Kelton cemetery	56	Church of the Good Shepherd, Ogden	78
Kelton marker	57	Corinne map, 1871	79
Camp Victory, Hart	59	Corinne pioneer railroad town sign	79
10-Mile marker	59	Trains at Corinne Railroad Museum	79
Train crew at 10-Mile marker	60	Presbyterian church, Corinne	80
Gap Between, Hart	60	Presbyterian bell, Corinne	80
Officials at Golden Spike ceremony	61	Presbyterian church centennial plaque	80
Post Office, Promontory Summit	61	Methodist Episcopal church, Ogden	81
Promontory Summit	61	Methodist Church sign, Corinne	82
Locomotive No. 119	62	Methodist church, Corinne	82
Central Pacific Railroad rolling stock	62	Ogden Academy	82
Gap in Rail	63	Burial vaults	84
Smokestack of the Jupiter	63	The 1897 Pioneer Days Parade	84
Jupiter with ties	63	*Harper's Weekly* cartoon	85
The Jupiter	64	Library of Congress cartoon	85
The last rail	64	Nitroglycerin plant, Richmond	85
The last spike with horses	65	Ogden cemetery	86
The last spike with army	65	Cathedral of the Madeleine	86
Union Pacific passenger cars	66	St. Patrick's Catholic church	86
Union Pacific workers	66	Holy Trinity	88
Central Pacific workers	67	Japanese Christian church	89
Flag	67	Buddhist temple	89
Laying the last rail	68	Undriven	90
The Jupiter, Promontory Summit	68	Replica engines	90

INTRODUCTION

While the railroad builders were not the first people in Utah, it probably seemed that way to those who arrived from the West. They encountered no settlements before arriving at Promontory Summit. Those coming from the East entered through the Mormon communities in the Echo and Weber canyons and then the Mormon and Shoshone communities along the Wasatch Front up to Brigham City. Heading west from there, they also encountered no settlements before meeting the builders from the West at Promontory Summit. Driving the Golden Spike there on May 10, 1869, opened Utah to the world.

The completion of the Transcontinental Railroad was a great achievement, but the first passengers did not arrive in San Francisco from Omaha until September 6, 1869. Those months between May and September were spent doing repairs and reinforcements to the tracks and building station houses to accommodate the services and safety required for passenger travel.

1

HISTORY

The first known settlers were the Native American tribes of the Great Basic Desert Archaic Period, as early as 12,000 BCE, followed by the Fremont Culture from about 400 CE. They were followed about 1300 CE by the Western Shoshone, Goshute, Ute, Paiute, and Navaho peoples who still live in this area today.

The first non-native explorers arrived in Utah with the Spanish explorers of the Juan Maria Antonia Rivera expedition in 1768, followed by the Dominguez and Escalante expedition in 1776. They were just passing through, making maps from New Mexico to Monterey, California.

Hunters, trappers, and their guides from all over North America also passed through the area before 1800 to obtain animals and their furs. They were followed by a series of government agents who worked to monitor and assist the Indian tribes in this region. Some of these guides, like Jedediah Smith and Jim Bridger, are recognizable. Jedediah Smith was leading fur trappers through Utah as early as 1824. That same year, Jim Bridger reported sighting the Great Salt Lake.

The first maps of the area were made by these early explorers, giving a rough path for companies of pioneer settlers in wagon trains to travel through the area. The first of these was the 1841 Bidwell–Bartleson Party of seventy-seven, including fifteen women and children. The path they cleared went across the top of the Great Salt Lake into Humboldt Wells, Nevada. It was the same route later followed by the Transcontinental Railroad through that area. The Donner–Reed Party also crossed Northern Utah, although on a slightly different route, in 1846.

The first settlement was Fort Buenaventura, built by Miles Goodyear, a mountain man, in 1844–1845 near the location that is now Ogden. He sold it to the newly arrived Mormons in 1847.

The Transcontinental Railroad in Utah

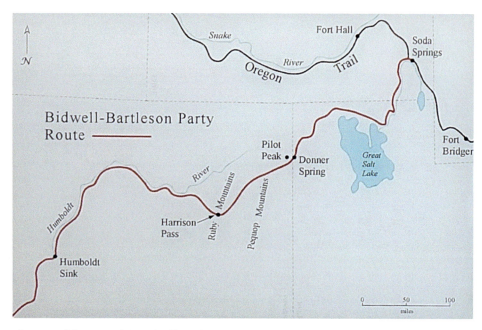

This map of the route of the Bidwell–Bartleson wagon train across the top of the Great Salt Lake and down to Humboldt Wells, Nevada, is displayed at the California Emigrant Trail Interpretive Center, Elko, Nevada.

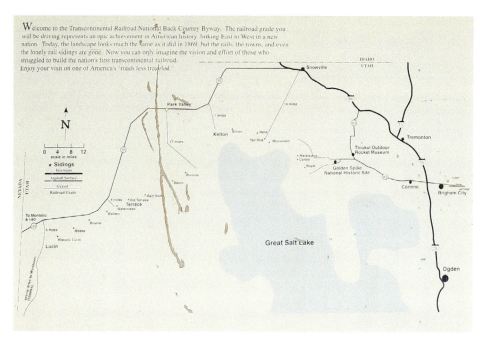

This map of Transcontinental Railroad from the Nevada border to Ogden is posted by the Bureau of Land Management (BLM).

History

Echo Canyon

Historic Corridor

Modern roads and highways often follow historic transportation corridors. In the mid 1800s, the California, Mormon Pioneer, and Pony Express Trails all passed through this canyon. Today, Interstate 80 in Echo Canyon follows the same historic route.

The Canyon Remembers

Sounds of travelers have lingered between these red canyon walls for hundreds of years. Sometimes, if you listen closely, through the din of today's auto and truck traffic you may hear the echoes of our past:

- the scraping of native Ute and Shoshone travois on river gravel,
- the crunch of fur trapper's footsteps in the snow,
- the whinnying, braying, and bellowing of horses, mules, and oxen,
- the crack of a teamster's whip,
- the creaking of wagons and stagecoaches,
- and the chugging, hissing, and clickity-clack of a steam locomotive on rails.

Walking next to an ox-drawn wagon in 1847, it took two days to get here from the Wyoming border. By Overland Stage in 1859, the trip took over three hours. By train in 1870, the distance was covered in just under two hours. How long did it take you today?

A UDOT ENHANCEMENT PROJECT SPONSORED BY THE UTAH HISTORIC TRAILS CONSORTIUM

This map of the Pony Express trail through Echo Canyon is an UDOT enhancement project sponsored by the Utah Historic Trails Corsortium.

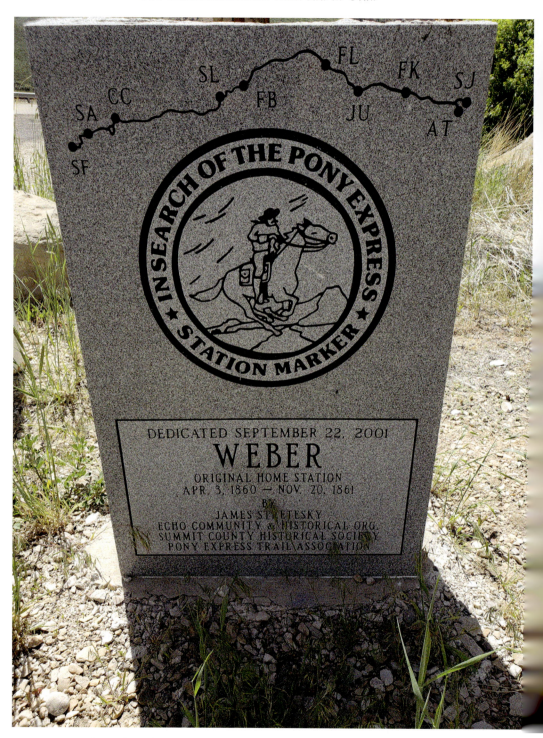

Pony Express marker at the Weber Station. (*Author's collection*)

2

RELIGIOUS GROUPS

LATTER-DAY SAINTS (LDS, MORMON)

The Mormon settlers arrived in 1847 after fleeing Carthage, Missouri, to more freely practice their religion. They were primarily farmers and did not encourage other groups to settle among them. Yet they did encourage and assist Mormon converts in their move to Utah. While they had a common religion, they were originally a mixture of several different western European ethnic groups.

The 1870 census showed 24 percent of Utah's population were from the British Isles, mostly as a result of the LDS British Mission, converting and moving those converts to Utah since 1837.

The first German settler in Utah arrived in 1847 as part of the first company of LDS pioneers. More LDS German immigrants followed, including those hired to work in the Tintic Mining District in the 1870s, along with Cornish, Welsh, Finnish, and Irish miners.

The first Swedish immigrant to Utah was a member of the Mormon battalion. This unit was recruited in Council Bluffs, Iowa, from among the Mormon pioneers headed west, to fight in the Mexican–American War. They served from July 1846 to July 1847, marching nearly 2,000 miles to San Diego, California in the course of their service. While some stayed in California, most rejoined their families who had founded Salt Lake City in 1847.

In 1852–1853, he returned to Sweden where he converted and then traveled with nearly 300 Swedish immigrants to Utah. More than 2,000 people followed this example in each decade from the 1860s through the 1880s. The early arrivals were farmers while later arrivals were merchants and miners, often not LDS.

Danish Mormons were among the earliest arrivals in Utah (1852). By 1890, 10 percent of Utah's population was either born in Denmark or a child of parents born in Denmark. Some of the first settlers in Brigham City were Danish converts recently arrived from Denmark. Other Danish converts settled in Manti, Ephraim, and Mount Pleasant. The Scandinavian Festival in Ephraim every year welcomes everyone to learn about their heritage.

Brigham City was settled by three LDS families in 1851. In 1853, a LDS group of fifty families moved into the area, including many immigrant farmers from Denmark.

The town was surveyed and named in 1855. Small businesses were established while the courthouse was used for theatrical and religious meetings as well as city and county (Box elder) business.

Swiss immigrants started arriving in Utah in the 1850s, mostly Mormon converts engaged in farming. They settled in groups in Santa Clara, Midway, Providence, and Logan. Other Swiss immigrant families were scattered in many communities in Utah. "Swiss Days" is a popular celebration of this heritage each year in Midway.

Hollander immigrants started arriving in Utah in 1860, primarily as Mormon converts. They settled mostly in Ogden and Salt Lake City, primarily as farmers.

South Sea Islanders started arriving in Utah in 1875 as Mormon converts. In 1889, they formed a colony in the desert of Skull Valley they named Iosepa. It was an agricultural community until about 1915 when an LDS temple in Hawaii encouraged their return to their homes in Hawaii and other Pacific islands.

The Mormons saw the railroad as a means to increase the migration of their converts to join them in Utah. Their support for the railroad is clearly seen in the lives of the families of Brigham Young, his sons, and other LDS leaders. Once the Transcontinental Railroad was completed, many other railroad lines crossed Utah from Idaho to Arizona and from Colorado to Nevada.

Above left: Oldest Mormon building in Ogden, the LDS 3rd Ward was built in 1856. (*Stewart Library Weber State University, Ogden, UT*)

Above right: Iosepa cemetery. (*Author's collection*)

Religious Groups

JEWISH

Julius and Fanny Brooks arrived in Salt Lake City from Frankenstein, Germany, in 1853, but moved on to California after one winter. However, they returned in 1864, opening a hat shop. More Jewish merchants arrived in 1857 to provide goods at the new U.S. Army Camp Floyd, south of Salt Lake City. The same year, Samuel Auerbach and Samuel Kahn arrived from California to set up department stores in Salt Lake City. Most of these early Jewish arrivals were of German, Russian, or Hungarian birth (according to the census records). Actually, they all immigrated to the United States from the Pale of Settlement area in Eastern Europe, including the countries named above.

There was a row of stores housed in tents at Promontory Summit in 1870. In the center of the photo below is G. Goldberg selling liquor and tobacco. In 1870, he appeared on the census in Corinne, Utah. In 1880, the census showed him living in Ogden, Utah. The *Helena Weekly Herald* newspaper ran his obituary in 1881, showing that his wife was from that area where her brothers were also merchants and that he had also owned a store there.

An Auerbach Brothers (Samuel and Frederick) department store was established in Corinne, Utah in 1870, visible in the photo below. Comments have been made about the absence of a Jewish Synagogue in Utah until later, but worship is often practiced in the home when there is only a small community. These early merchants often had stores in several towns and traveled a lot in the course of their businesses.

Note the Goldberg store in this photo of a row of merchant tents next to the railroad track at Promontory Summit, Utah about 1870, part of the display at the Golden Spike National Historic Site at Promontory Summit, Utah.

This photo of a street of merchant tent stores in Corinne, Utah, about 1871 is displayed at the Corinne "Hell on Wheels" display.

Religious Groups

This census page shows a great variety of nationalities and occupations in homes in Corinne, Utah in the 1870 U.S. Census. (*National Archives and Records Administration*)

This census page shows a street of hotels and boarding houses containing a great variety of nationalities and occupations in Ogden, Utah in 1870, U.S. Census. (*NARA*)

Simon Bamberger was listed on the 1870 census owning a hotel in Ogden (see image on p. 18). He lived In Salt Lake City on the 1880 census. He was born in Hesse-Darmstadt (a German state). He was a Jewish man who was very successful in Utah politics, becoming governor in 1916. His success was due in part to a nominating speech by LDS Apostle Brigham H. Roberts, despite an anti-Semitic campaigning against him. He supported Liberty Bond drives during World War I, mine taxes, compulsory high school attendance, and women's suffrage. He did not run for a second term and died of a heart attack in 1926.

CATHOLIC

General Patrick Edward Connor was born in Ireland. He moved to and worked in New York City before joining the U.S. Army in 1838 at the age of eighteen. During the Mexican–American War, he joined a company of Texas volunteers and was noted for his courage and military skill. In 1850, he was in California, settling at the mouth of the Trinity River. In 1853, he joined a company of California Rangers commissioned to hunt down the bandits led by Joaquin Murrieta. The next year, he married and settled in Stockton, California. He volunteered for the Union Army in the Civil War and was appointed to the rank of colonel. His duties were to guard the mail route across the West, so he moved his company to Salt Lake City, Utah, in 1862, founding Fort Douglas. His actions against the various Indian tribes earned him the rank of general. He was finally discharged as a brevet major-general in 1866. He stayed in Utah to promote mining activity, actively encouraging non-Mormons to work and live in Utah. He is remembered as the "Father of Utah mining" and the founder of the anti-Mormon "liberal party."

Father Lawrence Scanlon was entrusted with the care of the Catholic population of Utah in 1873. Born in Ireland, he was perceived as the Irish influence in the community, building churches, schools, and hospitals at railroad junctions, starting with Salt Lake City and Ogden in 1875. He became bishop in 1891, overseeing the new Salt Lake City Diocese whose population had grown from 800 to 8,000 in that time. The people of Irish origin shown in the 1870 census in Utah were mostly involved in trade and mining and usually Catholic, including General Patrick Edward Connor. The first Catholic church in Utah was completed in 1909 in Salt Lake City and under the patronage of St. Mary Magdalene.

The Sisters of the Holy Cross opened the Sacred Heart Academy at Washington Blvd and 26th Street in Ogden in 1878. The original enrollment was 150 day students and sixty resident students. By 1892, they had outgrown the building and moved to Quincy Ave and 25th Street in Ogden.

The 1860 census shows the country of birth, revealing the diversity of Utah's primarily Mormon population. There were Australians (ten), Austrians (fifty-one), Canadians (647), and one man from China. It also showed people from Denmark (1,824), England (7,084), France (twenty-one), and Germany (107). Also living here were people from Ireland (278), Italy (forty), Mexico (twelve), with one from the Netherlands. Among them were people from Norway (159), Poland (two), Portugal (one), Sardinia (nineteen, today we would add them to the Italian population), Scotland (1,228), Spain (five), Sweden (196), Switzerland (seventy-eight), and Wales (945). Some were listed as "Other Great Britain" (five), "Other Africa" (seventeen), "Other Europe" (two), and "Other" (ten). These totaled a foreign-born population of 12,754 out of a total population of 40,273.

Left: Monument to General Connor at Fort Douglas Military Post Cemetery, Salt Lake City, Utah. (*Author's collection*)

Below: Sacred Heart Academy in Ogden. (*Stewart Library, Weber State University, Ogden, Utah*)

3

BUILDING THE RR

The Transcontinental Railroad was meant as a unifying tool for the country, with the first discussions in 1832 in the Ann Arbor, Michigan *The Emigrant* newspaper. It was also part of U.S. Presidential Campaigns in 1852, 1856, and 1860. It was passed as law with the Pacific Railroad Act signed by President Lincoln in 1862. The actual title of this Act is "An Act to Aid in the Construction of a Railroad and Telegraph line from the Missouri River to the Pacific Ocean, and to secure to the Government the use of the same for postal, military and other purposes."

This enabled the builders of the Transcontinental Railroad to post their progress, order supplies, and alert oncoming traffic to dangers ahead by use of the telegraph running next to their rails.

Travelers to the western gold fields in California and other destinations could only travel 10–12 miles a day in wagons pulled by oxen. That increased to 15–25 miles a day if the wagons were pulled by horses. That increased to 100–150 miles a day when taking the stagecoach. The railroad increased that to 300 miles a day. The advantages were obvious.

Building the railroad required a lot of money and manpower. The route had been planned by surveyors, mostly following old trapper, pioneer, Pony Express, and pioneer wagon train trails. The goal was the most moderate grade (uphill and downhill angles) and minimal bridges and tunnels while establishing the most direct (fastest) route.

Railroad work camps often turned into train stations, placed 10–12 miles apart to fill water tanks for the steam engines as well as add fuel, freight, and passengers.

Time zones had not been standardized when the railroad building began. In fact, there were over 100 time zones in the United States, each with local authority. The arrival of the Transcontinental Railroad led to the standardized time zones we use today.

The Transcontinental Railroad in Utah

The telegraph accompanied the railroad across the country, as legislated by Congress, panel by National Park Service at Golden Spike National Historic Site.

4

THE TRANSCONTINENTAL RAILROAD ROUTE THROUGH UTAH

UNION PACIFIC RAILROAD

The Union Pacific Railroad started west from Omaha, Nebraska with crews composed mostly of Civil War veterans, mostly Irish, English, and German immigrants, Native Americans, and freed African-American slaves. They were running coal-burning steam engines. The crews lived in train cars built as dormitories with three-tiered bunks and different cars for dining and storage. They were accompanied by a herd of cattle used for food along the way.

In Utah, particularly at Echo and Weber Canyons and at Big Fill (just east of Promontory Summit), they used Mormon crews to supplement the manpower of the Union Pacific Railroad crews. In the canyons, this was because the land mostly belonged to Mormons who provided the crews. At Big Fill, it was a matter of getting the job done in the shortest time to enable passenger travel on the track there. The trestle had been built to speed the completion of the line, but clearly was not safe enough for more than temporary use.

Big Fill replaced Big Trestle just east of Promontory Summit to level the space for the railroad tracks. The photos are spectacular since they show with railroad cars and people just how deep that chasm was before getting filled.

These are photos of the construction of the Union Pacific Railroad from Omaha to Utah and are by Andrew J. Russell.

The descriptions of the landmarks and stops from the Wyoming border to Promontory Summit are described here as follows:

Wahsatch
This railroad stop and repair station was noted on maps from 1876, 1883, and 1900. Wahsatch began as a Union Pacific Railroad camp with the building of the Transcontinental Railroad and became a center of sheep ranching until the 1930s when it was abandoned.

Above: Union Pacific Railroad construction at Chemin de Fer.

Below: Trestle at Dale Creek.

The Transcontinental Railroad Route Through Utah

Above: Citadel Rock and Bridge near Green River, WY, 1868.

Below: Main street, Bear River City, WY, 1868.

The Transcontinental Railroad in Utah

Above: Mezzanine, note the railroad ties stacked along the rail bed.

Below: Railroad workers with shovels line the track with the water boy front and center, an essential part of the work crew.

The Transcontinental Railroad Route Through Utah

Above: Union Pacific Construction train near Ogden, 1868. These trains provided materials as well as living quarters for the crews.

Below: Andrew J. Russell documented the project, marking 1,000 miles of rail laid from Omaha, Nebraska by Union Pacific Railroad crews at this tree with his photograph.

Railroad stations from Wyoming to Promontory are shown on this section of an 1876 Rand McNally map in the Library of Congress.

Train moving through Echo Canyon today. (*Author's collection*)

The Transcontinental Railroad Route Through Utah

Wahsatch in about 1870. (*Utah State Historical Society*)

Wahsatch today is still a maintenance point for railroad repairs. (*Author's collection*)

The Transcontinental Railroad in Utah

Castle Rock
This railroad stop noted on maps from 1876, 1883, and 1900 is a ghost town with abandoned buildings and livestock corrals.

Emory
Also known as Hanging Rock for the geological formation near this railroad stop, it was noted on maps from 1876 and 1900.

Echo
This railroad stop in the town of the same name was noted on maps in 1876, 1883, and 1900. The town began as a stage stop and became a stagecoach resting stop used by such notables as Lotta Crabtree and Mark Twain. In 1861, it was settled by a group of businessmen as a town to provide services to the increasing number of travelers passing through.

Croydon
Also known as Weber's Quarry, this railroad stop was noted on maps in 1876, 1883, and 1900. Croydon is still an unincorporated area, first settled in 1862.

Morgan
This railroad station was named for the town and noted on maps in 1883 and 1900. Morgan was first settled in 1860 as a farming community.

Peterson
This railroad stop was noted on maps in 1883 and 1900.

Strawberry
This railroad stop was noted on a 1900 map where Strawberry Creek crosses the rails.

Devil's Gate
This railroad stop was noted on an 1876 map at the geological formation of the same name.

Uintah
This railroad stop was noted on maps in 1876 and 1900. Uintah was first settled in 1850 by Mormon farmers, sharing the location with Shoshone Indians who lived in the area first.

Ogden
This railroad station was named for the city and noted on maps from 1876, 1883, and 1900. The city grew from the purchase of Fort Buenaventura in 1847. It was named the county seat of Weber County in 1850 and incorporated as a city in 1851. It was the city center of a farming community at a transportation hub. A grand celebration was held here to mark the arrival of the Union Pacific Railroad builders working toward the completion of the Transcontinental Railroad. Today, Ogden Station hosts several museums and is a center of community activity.

Above: Castle Rock today. See the lower railroad track to the far left, while above that same shack is the tunnel for the upper railroad track. (*Author's collection*)

Right: These roadside markers are the only remains of Emory as a train stop and a Pony Express stop. (*Author's collection*)

Historic markers on display in Echo, showing the history and old photos of the town. (*Author's collection*)

The old railroad track trestle is seen below the new one above the raft floating down the Weber River. (*Author's collection*)

Historic Morgan railroad station today. (*Author's collection*)

Above left: The sign for Peterson Cemetery is the only evidence that this is Peterson, formerly a train stop and now a residential area with few services. (*Author's collection*)

Above right: Uintah about 1870. (*Utah State Historical Society*)

Below: Uintah today. (*Author's collection*)

The Transcontinental Railroad Route Through Utah

This photo of the first railroad station at Ogden is on display at the Railroad Museum at Ogden Station.

This is one of the first trains to stop at the Ogden station, on display at the Railroad Museum at Ogden.

View of Ogden in 1876. (*Stewart Library, Weber State University*)

Ogden railroad station. (*Author's collection*)

The Transcontinental Railroad Route Through Utah

South Willard
Also known as Bonneville, this was a railroad station noted on maps from 1876, 1883, and 1900. This area is still unincorporated, and started as a farming community expansion of Willard City.

Willard City
This railroad stop was noted on maps from 1876 and is named for the city. Willard was founded in 1851 as a farming community.

Brigham City
This railroad station was noted on maps from 1876, 1883, and 1900 and was named for the city. Brigham City was founded in 1851 as a farming community.

Corinne
Also known as Bear River, this railroad station was noted on maps from 1876, 1883, and 1900, and was named for the city. Corinne was founded in 1869 by military veterans and non-Mormon businessmen in anticipation of the coming Transcontinental Railroad.

Stokes
This railroad stop was noted by the Bureau of Land Management historians as a freight stop. It was also noted in the 1922 edition of *Bullinger's Postal and Shippers Guide for the United States and Canada*.

Balfour
This railroad stop was noted by the Bureau of Land Management historians as a freight stop. It was also listed in the 1903–1904 *Utah State Gazetteer and Business Directory*.

Connor
This railroad stop noted by the Bureau of Land Management historians as a freight stop near Connor Springs.

Blue Creek
This railroad stop was noted by the Bureau of Land Management historians. This stop was near Promontory Summit, where the Blue Creek crosses the railroad tracks. The current town with this name is further north on the same creek.

Lampo
This railroad stop was noted by the Bureau of Land Management historians as a freight stop. This location is described in more detail at boxeldercounty.org/lampo.htm.

Surbon
This railroad stop was noted by the Bureau of Land Management historians as a freight stop.

Willard cemetery sign. (*Author's collection*)

Brigham City railroad station has been restored and houses a nice museum today. (*Author's collection*)

The Transcontinental Railroad Route Through Utah

This photo is of construction at Bear River, photo by Andrew J. Russell as part of his documentation of the building of the Transcontinental Railroad by the Union Pacific.

The Daughters of Utah Pioneers marked the location of the Corinne Opera House to preserve that piece of history.

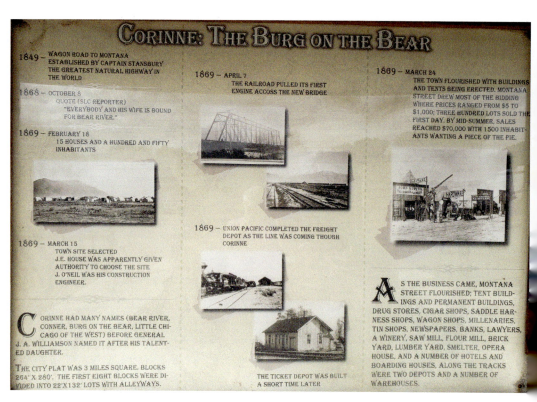

These two information posters at Corinne show the history of the area. (*Author's collection*)

The Transcontinental Railroad Route Through Utah

Today's town of Blue Creek is further north, but where the creek crosses the tracks is the location of this train stop. Map is from Golden Spike National Historic Site, run by the National Park Service.

Big Trestle and Big Fill
An engineering milestone lies near Promontory Summit, known as Big Trestle and Big Fill. It started out as Big Trestle, a quickly erected way for the train to cross the area. However, this was an unstable erection, so with the assistance of local Mormon farmers in addition to the crews of both railroads, it was replaced by the Big Fill, leveling out the area so that safer travel was possible.

CENTRAL PACIFIC RAILROAD

The Central Pacific Railroad started East from Sacramento, California with crews who often didn't stay on the job due to the lure of the gold fields. This problem was solved by hiring Chinese crews (estimates run as high as 11,000 men), using experienced Irish foremen. They were running wood-burning steam engines. The Chinese crews lived in tents provided by the railroad, although they usually preferred to live in dugouts. They had a different diet than the Irish foremen who worked with them, with more fresh vegetables, rice, and tea. They had to pay for these special foods out of their wages, unlike the other employees. The camps did not allow drinking, unlike the Union Pacific Railroad camps, which were notorious for their liquor consumption. These crews had more tunnels on their route than the Union Pacific Railroad crews and used gunpowder, dynamite, and nitroglycerin to blast through the rock, sometimes leading to avalanches in the snowy Sierra Nevada mountain range, leading to more work injuries and deaths. Native Americans joined the work crews in Nevada and Utah. The Central Pacific Railroad hired Alfred A. Hart to document the construction with photographs, many of which are displayed here, thanks to the expired copyright and the National Park Service.

Photos from Sacramento to the Nevada border, by Alfred A. Hart, are seen here.

The landmarks and stops along this route from the Nevada border to Promontory Summit are described here as follows:

The Transcontinental Railroad in Utah

Above: Photo of the Big Trestle by Andrew J. Russell, from the NPS display at Golden Spike National Historic Site, run by the National Park Service.

Left: Photo of the Big Fill, from the National Park Service display at Golden Spike National Historic Site.

An Army of mostly Mormon laborers helped the Central Pacific overcome one of its last obstacles in the historic race to unite the states by rail.

As shown in the photo above, workers used small dumpcarts to haul 10,000 cubic yards of dirt into the Spring Creek ravine. This job took 500 men two intense months of work, but it saved the Central Pacific from having to dig a time- and money-consuming, 800-foot-long tunnel into the face of the Promontory Mountains.

The Transcontinental Railroad Route Through Utah

Above: Blasting a tunnel through the mountains.

Right: Railroad crews building a trestle.

The Transcontinental Railroad in Utah

American River at the foot of Cape Horn, 1,400 feet below, 1869.

Chinese crews using horse-drawn carts to bring in the dirt for a fill to level the grade for the tracks.

The Transcontinental Railroad Route Through Utah

Above: Construction also required repair crews who could replace both ties and rails.

Right: This drawing is of coaling on the road at Wannemacker by Chinese laborers, showing the use of coal as well as wood-burning steam engines on the Central Pacific Railroad portion of the line.

Above: This group of railroad workers is posing with the tools required in their work.

Left: The tracks required not only tunnels, but also snow galleries on the sides of mountains as shown here.

The Transcontinental Railroad Route Through Utah

Truckee depot, Truckee, California 1869. Note the multiple engines all steaming with their wood fuel cars and the tent city on the right.

Central Pacific Railroad workers showing how the grading of the track bed was achieved. (*Alfred A. Hart*)

Alfred A. Hart captured this photo of a Chinese railroad camp. (*National Park Service*)

Another Alfred A. Hart photo, showing a track laying crew of Chinese men.

The Transcontinental Railroad Route Through Utah

This map of railroad stations/stops from the Nevada border to Promontory Summit was created by the Chinese Railroad Workers in North America Project at Stanford University, a traveling exhibit.

This is the warning posted near the eastern entrance to the Bureau of Land Management Transcontinental Railroad Back Country Byway near Promontory Summit.

This is the marker posted at the western entrance to the Bureau of Land Management Transcontinental Railroad Back Country Byway near Lucin.

Umbria Junction
This railroad stop was noted by the Bureau of Land Management historians as a freight stop between 1899 and 1906. It is located between Lucin and the Nevada border.

Old Lucin
Also called Historic Lucin, it was renamed Grouse in 1905 after the Lucin Cut-Off shifted the population a few miles south. It was a railroad stop noted by the Bureau of Land Management historians between 1875 and 1907, noted on maps in 1883 and 1900.

Medea
This railroad stop was noted by the Bureau of Land Management historians as a freight stop from 1899–1906.

Bovine
This railroad stop was noted by the Bureau of Land Management historians as a freight stop from 1869–1905, noted on maps in 1900.

Walden
This railroad stop was noted by the Bureau of Land Management historians as a freight stop from 1898–1906.

Watercress
This railroad stop was noted by the Bureau of Land Management historians as a freight stop from 1910–1940.

Terrace
This railroad stop was noted by the Bureau of Land Management historians from 1869–1910, noted on maps from 1883 and 1900.

Red Dome
This railroad stop was noted by the Bureau of Land Management historians as a freight stop from 1895–1907.

Matlin
This railroad stop was noted by the Bureau of Land Management historians from 1869–1904, noted on maps in 1900.

Romola
This railroad stop noted by the Bureau of Land Management historians as a freight stop from 1899–1906.

Gravel Pit
This railroad stop was noted by the Bureau of Land Management historians as a construction camp from 1869–1901.

The Transcontinental Railroad Route Through Utah

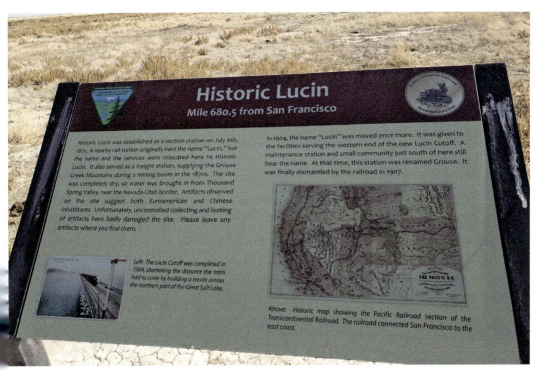

This information posted by the Bureau of Land Management at Old Lucin clearly stands alone in this desolate place. This area is known as the West Desert by Utahns and is also part of the Great Basin Desert geographical region, one of only four geographically defined deserts in North America (along with the Mojave, Sonoran, and Chihuahuan). (*Author's collection*)

The Transcontinental Railroad in Utah

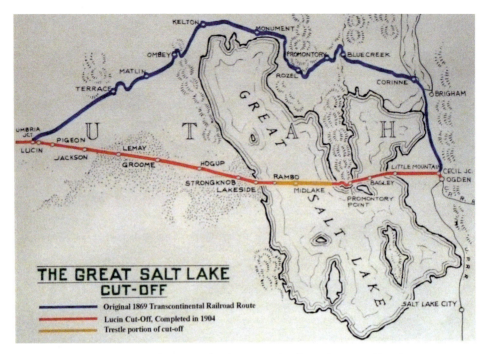

Above: Lucin cut-off map, from the National Park Service. This shows the new rail line from Lucin across the Great Salt Lake, making the old stops between Lucin and Corinne of little value until the rails were finally removed as "Undriven", part of the World War II metal recycling program.

Below: There is a Bureau of Land Management marker here at Watercress to pinpoint the site of the old town, although the rubble of the abandoned town is quite obvious. (*Author's collection*)

The Transcontinental Railroad Route Through Utah

Right: This culvert near Watercress still holds the original bolts. (*Author's collection*)

Below: Trestle located between Watercress and Terrace. (*Author's collection*)

Sign to Watercress and Terrace, pointing off the paved road. (*Author's collection*)

Terrace train station, from Utah State Historical Society.

This Bureau of Land Management marker shows the history and location of Terrace. This town was larger than Watercress and the remains of the destroyed town cover a large area. (*Author's collection*)

Ombey
This railroad stop was noted by the Bureau of Land Management historians from 1878–1910, noted on maps from 1900.

Peplin
This railroad stop was noted by the Bureau of Land Management historians as a freight stop from 1888–unknown.

Zias
This railroad stop was noted by the Bureau of Land Management historians as a freight stop from 1902–1906.

Kelton
This railroad stop was noted by the Bureau of Land Management historians from 1869–1942, noted on maps from 1883 and 1900.

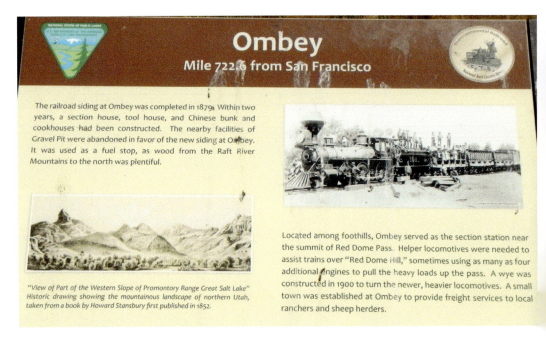

Ombey marker posted by Bureau of Land Management to show the history of the location.

Kelton cemetery. (*Author's collection*)

The Transcontinental Railroad Route Through Utah

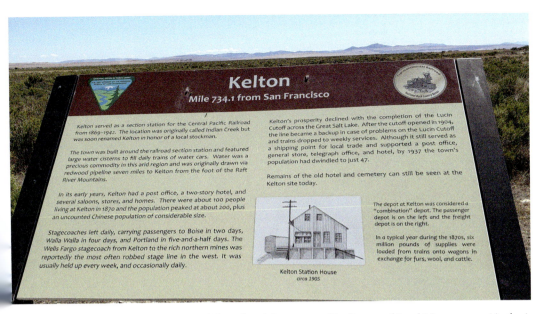

Kelton marker contains a drawing of the railroad depot, posted by Bureau of Land Management. (*Author's collection*)

Elinor
This railroad stop was noted by the Bureau of Land Management historians as a freight stop from 1902–1907.

Seco
This railroad stop was noted by the Bureau of Land Management historians as a freight stop from 1873–1901, noted on maps in 1900.

Nella
This railroad stop was noted by the Bureau of Land Management historians as a freight stop from 1902–1906 and 1916–unknown.

Ten-Mile Station
This railroad stop was noted by the Bureau of Land Management historians as a freight stop from 1869–1873. This location was named thusly because it was 10 miles from Lake Station.

Monument
This railroad stop was noted by the Bureau of Land Management historians from 1869–1942, noted on maps in 1883 and 1900.

East Kosmo
This railroad stop noted by the Bureau of Land Management historians as a freight stop from 1901–1906.

The Transcontinental Railroad in Utah

West Kosmo
This railroad stop was noted by the Bureau of Land Management historians as a freight stop from 1912–1942.

East Lake
This railroad stop was noted by the Bureau of Land Management historians from 1869–1890.

West Lake
This railroad stop noted by the Bureau of Land Management historians from 1877–1910, noted on maps in 1900.

Metatarus
This railroad stop was noted by the Bureau of Land Management historians as a freight stop from 1898–1909.

Centre
This railroad stop was noted by the Bureau of Land Management historians as a freight stop from 1879–1890.

Rozel
Also known as Camp Victory, this railroad stop was noted by the Bureau of Land Management historians from 1869–1942, noted on maps in 1900.

10-Mile Marker
The rail contest won by the CPRR for the most rail laid in one day ended at this spot.

Promontory Summit
This railroad stop was noted by the Bureau of Land Management historians from 1869–1942, noted on maps in 1883 and 1900.

Golden Spike Ceremony
The race to the finish pushed both groups past the junction point, each hoping for the recognition that would lead to subsidies for their company. Both sets of rails are still visible at Promontory Summit.

The ceremony marking the completion of the Transcontinental Railroad took place at Promontory Summit on 10 May 1869. The Union Pacific Railroad hired Andrew J. Russell to photograph their construction. The following photos were taken by Russell at the ceremonies at Promontory Point the day of the Gold Spike Ceremony.

These photos are on display to explain railroad construction at the Golden Spike National Historic Site, part of the National Park Service.

East of the NHS site at Promontory Summit is a Bureau of Land Management Transcontinental Railroad Back Country Byway following the original track lines to Lucin (near the Nevada border). This road is marginal, and there are warnings to use a high-clearance four-wheel drive vehicle are at each end of the road, along with advice to carry a spare tire in case you find a stray spike, and plenty of water since there are no services anywhere along this 90-mile road with twenty sites with markers showing the history of each location with old photos and explanations.

The Transcontinental Railroad Route Through Utah

This Camp Victory photo by Alfred A. Hart is also the location of the station at Rozel.

The 10-mile marker at the end of the rail contest, now on display at the Golden Spike National Historic Site at Promontory Summit, safe from the elements in a glass case. (*Author's collection*)

Railroad crew at the 10-mile sign in the 1930s, on display at the Golden Spike National Historic Site at Promontory Summit. (*Author's collection*)

"Gap Between the Rails" photo documents the two sets of rails laid by the two Railroad companies in their quest for the subsidies that would go to the chosen line. These photos by Alfred A. Hart document the golden spike celebration.

The Transcontinental Railroad Route Through Utah

Officials and their wives at Golden Spike ceremony, posed by the Union Pacific Train.

Post Office at Promontory Summit, Utah, part of a line of tent stores.

Promontory Summit, Utah, note that it contains only the one line of tent stores running parallel to the railroad tracks.

Union Pacific Railroad locomotive #119 at the ceremonies at Promontory Summit, Utah.

Central Pacific Railroad rolling stock, not the empty rail below it, showing the duplication of effort by the two railroad companies at this location.

The Transcontinental Railroad Route Through Utah

A gap in the rail, awaiting the ceremonial laying of the last rails before the golden spike was driven.

Above left: View over the smokestack of the *Jupiter* as the last spike was driven.

Above right: The *Jupiter* with ties in the foreground.

The *Jupiter* (Central Pacific railroad engine) posing with an army band for the ceremony.

The last rail just before being laid on the track.

The Transcontinental Railroad Route Through Utah

Driving the last spike with the horses on the edge of the crowd and the Andrew J. Russell climbing a ladder against the flagpole to get a better shot of the ceremony.

The driving of the last spike, with the white-gloved army lined up between the two engines.

The Transcontinental Railroad in Utah

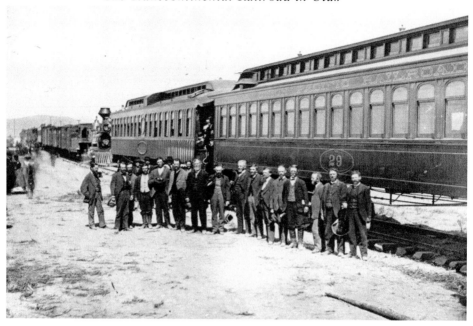

These Union Pacific passenger cars are pulled up so you can only see the Central Pacific locomotive engine facing them. The well-dressed men are some of the officials gathered for the event.

These Union Pacific Railroad workers are standing in front of the train cars they called home while building the railroad.

The Transcontinental Railroad Route Through Utah

These Central Pacific Railroad workers are sitting on the fuel car, showing the wood used for fuel in their steam engine.

The flagpole dominates this scene with the two engines facing each other and the ladies front and center of the group posing as the photographer climbs the ladder to get the best shot.

The Transcontinental Railroad in Utah

Above: This view of the last rail shows the white-gloved army lined up as well as the ladies and children standing on the rail in front of the Union Pacific Locomotive.

Below: This photo of the Central Pacific Railroad locomotive (the *Jupiter*) facing the Union Pacific locomotive with dignitaries at the ceremonies at Promontory Summit.

The Transcontinental Railroad Route Through Utah

Above: This is the iconic photo of the celebration when the Transcontinental Railroad was complete.

Above left: The directors of the railroad companies in a meeting room railroad car.

Above right: This broader view of the last rail being laid shows the train on the other track and some of the wagons and other people who attended the event.

The Transcontinental Railroad in Utah

This photo of the last rail ceremony clearly shows the Chinese and Irish workers of both the Central Pacific Railroad and the Union Pacific Railroad working together to get the job done.

The Union Pacific officials were a day late to Promontory Summit because they needed to pay their workers; here, they await the paymaster.

The Transcontinental Railroad Route Through Utah

Right: This ad for the Union and Central Pacific Railroad line shows departure from three cities: Omaha, Nebraska to Cheyenne, Wyoming; St. Joseph, Missouri to Ogden, Utah; and Kansas City, Missouri to Denver, Colorado. From these cities, the route goes to San Francisco, Portland, and all points in California, Nevada, Oregon, Washington, and British Columbia. This shows how quickly other railroads lines were built off the original Transcontinental Railroad.

Below: Competition 1869 maps the railbed built by the competing Union Pacific and Central Pacific running past each other near Promontory Summit in a bid for the funding awarded the company whose track was chosen for the meeting. It is displayed at Golden Spike National Historic Site.

Great curved trestle at Secrettown, 62 miles from Sacramento. Chinese laborers with horse-drawn carts are dwarfed by the trestle, 1868.

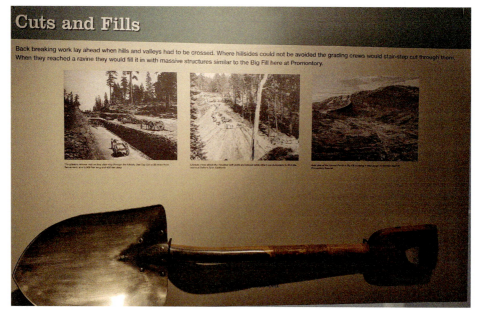

"Cuts and Fills" with a shovel display photos of different approaches to creating a grade optimal for the railroad.

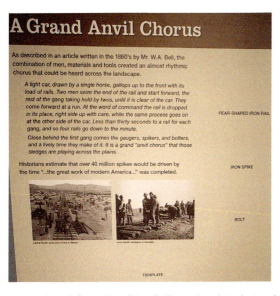
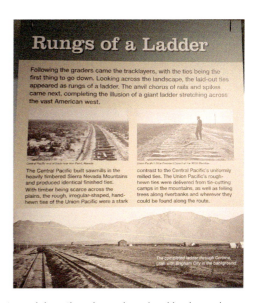

Above left: "A Grand Anvil Chorus" explains laying the ties and the rail on the grade sculpted by the workmen before them.

Above right: "Rungs of a Ladder" shows photos of the ties in place before the rails were laid, as well as a photo of the rail line running through Corinne, removed during World War II.

Below left: "Tunnels and Trestles" explains how the tunnels were unstable and had to be reinforced with timber. The trestles were considered temporary until they could be replaced by fills or permanent (more stable) bridges.

Below right: This ad placed 10 May 1869 to promote the grand opening of the Union Pacific from the Atlantic to the Pacific via Omaha and through to San Francisco in fewer than four days. It also shows connections at Cheyenne for Denver, Central City, and Sante Fe. There were also connections from Ogden and Corinne to Helena, Virginia City, Salt Lake City, and Arizona.

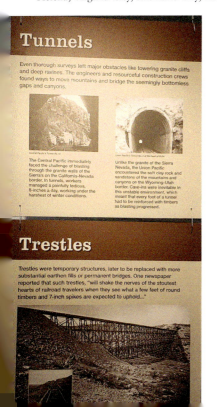
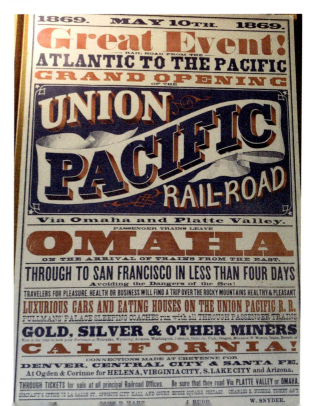

The Transcontinental Railroad in Utah

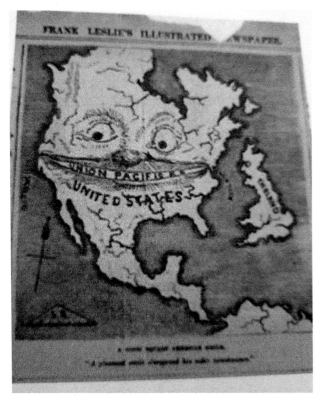

These two cartoons were published in Frank Leslie's *Illustrated Newspaper* in 1869 to celebrate the completion of the Transcontinental Railroad.

The Transcontinental Railroad Route Through Utah

Right: The Chinese Historical Society of America placed this marker to recognize the Chinese Railroad Workers on the Transcontinental Railroad. (*Author's collection*)

Below: The Hibernian Society of Utah placed this marker to recognize the Irish Railroad Workers on the Transcontinental Railroad. (*Author's collection*)

The Transcontinental Railroad in Utah

This Union Pacific Railroad Train stopped at Ogden, displayed by National Park Service at Golden Spike National Historic Site at Promontory Summit, Utah.

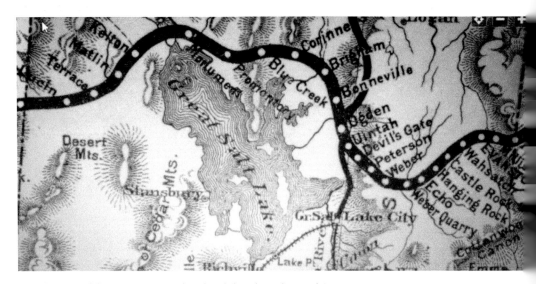

An 1883 map of the Transcontinental Railroad, found at Library of Congress.

5

PROTESTANTS

The completion of the Transcontinental Railroad brought evangelical Protestants into Utah. After the arrival of the railroad, schools and churches were established in Utah by Presbyterians, Methodists, Baptists, and Lutherans and others with the goal of reclaiming Mormons to their religions.

In 1865, the first non-Mormon religious services were held in Salt Lake City, conducted by Rev. Norman McLeod, a Congregational missionary. He is remembered as a spellbinding anti-Mormon preacher.

The first Episcopalian missionary arrived in Salt Lake City in 1867. In 1873, they built a school in Salt Lake City, later joined by a day and boarding school called Rowland Hall, still a part of the community today. The cornerstone for the Cathedral Church of St. Mark was laid in 1870. They built the school of the Good Shepherd in Ogden the same year for railroad families who did not want their children in Mormon schools. The cornerstone for the Church of the Good Shepherd in Ogden was laid in 1874. There was no hospital for injured miners and railroad workers until 1872 when they built St. Mark's Hospital in Salt Lake City.

There was a railroad museum at Corinne, which no longer exists; it is part of the section on Corinne.

Corinne was founded in 1869 by former Union Army officers and non-Mormon merchants from Salt Lake City. While this town had a reputation as a "hell-on-wheels" town along the railroad lines (lots of bars and lawlessness), there were Methodist, Presbyterian, Episcopalian, Baptist, and Catholic churches as well. The railroad lines between Salt Lake City and Idaho crossed the Transcontinental rail line at Ogden in 1877, decreasing the traffic to Corinne. Most of Corinne's merchants made the move to Ogden and the town gradually became the Mormon farming town it is today.

Corinne was home to the first Presbyterian minister in Utah in 1869, one month after the golden spike ceremony. In 1871, the first Presbyterian church in Salt Lake City was organized. Alta was home to this church with a school in 1873. Between 1877 and 1884, thirty-three schools were started. Also in 1870, the cornerstone was laid for the Methodist Episcopalian church, now owned by the city for museum and the oldest standing Protestant church in Utah.

Cathedral Church of Saint Mark in Salt Lake City, now also home of the Episcopal Diocese of Utah. (*Author's collection*)

Church of the Good Shepherd in Ogden. (*Stewart Library, Weber State University, Ogden, UT*)

 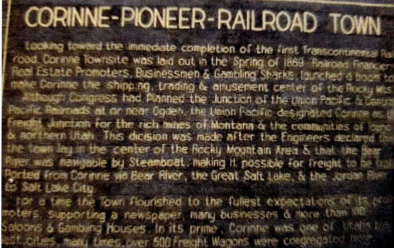

Above left: This map of Corinne in 1871 from the Golden Spike National Historic Site at Promontory shows churches built by Presbyterians, Methodists, Episcopalians, Catholics, and Baptists.

Above right: Corinne Pioneer Railroad Town sign. (*Author's collection*)

Below: This photo of two trains at the Railroad Museum at Corinne shows a Southern Pacific and a Union Pacific engine, neither one a steam engine. The railroad stock and other museum displays were sold off and the museum no longer exists. (*Utah State Historical Society*)

The Transcontinental Railroad in Utah

Above left: The Presbyterian church in Corinne founded in 1871. This photo is displayed at the Corinne "Hell on Wheels" display.

Above right: Bell from original Presbyterian church in Corinne.

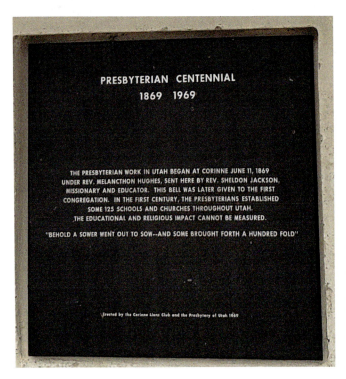

Left: Plaque commemorating 100 years of the Presbyterian Church in Corinne. (*Author's collection*)

Opposite: The First Presbyterian Church in Ogden was organized in 1878, with their first church built at 24th St and Lincoln Ave in 1880. (*Stewart Library, Weber State University, Ogden, UT*)

The First Methodist Episcopal Church of Ogden was organized in 1870, holding the first services at the Union and Central Pacific Railroad station. A new church was built in at 24th St., now a nightclub. In 1890, a new church was built at 26th Street and Jefferson Ave, in use today.

In 1870, the first Methodist church of Salt Lake City was organized, also a school. Later, other churches and schools were organized in Corinne, Tooele, Beaver, and Provo in Utah.

The first Baptist congregation was established in 1871 in Salt Lake City. A congregation was established in Ogden in 1881 by Rev. Dwight Spencer., building their first church at Grant Ave and 25th St.

Non-Mormons from Sweden arrived in greater numbers in the 1880s to work in the mines and mills. The Zion Swedish Lutheran church was established in Salt Lake City in 1881, primarily to convert Mormons. Most of these early Lutheran churches in Utah conducted services in languages that were not English.

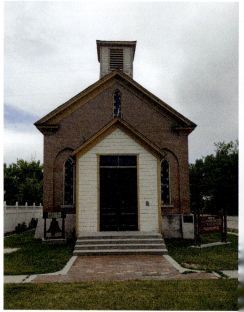

Above left: Corinne Methodist church sign. (*Author's collection*)

Above right: The Methodist church in Corinne, founded in 1870. (*Author's collection*)

Below: Some 600 student capacity at Ogden Academy, built by the Congregational church in 1887. (*Stewart Library, Weber State University, Ogden, UT*)

6

ETHNIC GROUPS

After the completion of the Transcontinental Railroad, large numbers of other groups made the move to Utah. The 1870 census showed the increase in not only population, but ethnic diversity in Utah. It listed foreign born as including people from Africa (128), Asia (sixteen), Australia (seventy-four), Austria (four), Belgium (two), Bohemia (three), Canada (687), China (446), Denmark (4,957), England (16,073), France (sixty-three), Germany (358), and one man from Greece. Other people were born in Hawaii (ten), Hungary (one), Ireland (502), Italy (seventy-four), Mexico (eight), Netherlands (122), Norway (613), Poland (eleven), Portugal (two), and Russia (thirteen). More people were born in Scotland (2,391), South America (three), Spain (two), Sweden (1,790), Switzerland (509), Wales (1,783), and the West Indies (three). There were also twenty-one born at sea plus "Other Great Britain" (twenty-three) and "Other Europe" (eight). The total foreign-born population was 30,702 out of a total population of 86,786.

Most Chinese people in Utah arrived with the railroad, although one was listed in the 1860 census. They never intended to stay, being sojourners who earned money to send home to their families until their return home. Wong Leung Ka arrived in Ogden around 1880, intending to return home. He was a successful businessman who lived in Ogden for forty-six years, visiting family in China on two occasions. His store sold groceries and items imported from China. There were sleeping rooms on the upper level. He was known for his compassion and generosity, providing meals and sleeping rooms for the unemployed who repaid him when they found work. Their organization of the annual "Golden Spike Reenactment" each May 10 celebrates the completion of the Transcontinental Railroad at Promontory Summit.

A significant number of Irish immigrants and their children were working on the railroad when they settled in Utah. Most of the train stations located every 10–12 miles was home to a crew of about ten Chinese workers and two Irish foremen. While steam engines needed fuel and water about every 30 miles, the tracks required constant maintenance. The railroad brought more people from Ireland to work in the mines as well as with the many railroads newly built in Utah. The Hibernian Society with its annual St. Patrick's Day parade is a vibrant part of Utah centered in Salt Lake City. The Cathedral of the Madeleine is a landmark in Salt Lake City with a much-appreciated music program.

These burial vaults contain the remains of Chinese residents of Salt Lake City Cemetery.

Photo of the 1897 Pioneer Days Parade in Salt Lake City with the Chinese dragon float progressing down the street.

Ethnic Groups

The anti-Chinese movement spread across the United States in the 1870s and 1880s. (Library of Congress)

Above left: Cartoon in *Harper's Weekly* by Thomas Nast in 1871 denouncing the treatment of the Chinese in America. Yet the conflict escalated and resulted in the Chinese Exclusion Act of 1882.

Above right: This cartoon from the Library of Congress dates from the anti-Chinese movement still strong in 1883. The Chinese Exclusion Act was not repealed until 1943 when we wanted the cooperation of China against the Japanese in World War II.

Chinese workers at nitroglycerin plant in Richmond, California, from the Collection of the Richmond Museum of History.

Above: The oldest-known Chinese burials in Utah are located at the Ogden Cemetery. (*Author's collection*)

Below left: The Cathedral of the Madeleine in Salt Lake City was built in 1909, but was originally an Irish parish started in 1871. It is also the home of the Diocese of Salt Lake City, within the Ecclesiastical Province of San Francisco. (*Christine Saffell*)

Below right: St. Patrick's Catholic Church was built in 1916 in the "Little Italy" neighborhood of Salt Lake City. (*Author's collection*)

Ethnic Groups

There were a few free people of African heritage along with a few slaves living in Utah before the 1870 census when they numbered 118. Their numbers increased to 677 in 1900 due to the railroad, mining, and military employment opportunities. Today, this community is an integral part of Utah and they are joyfully heard and seen in the annual Pioneer Day Parade in Salt Lake City where the choirs of several Baptist Churches are enjoyed by all.

The first Italian immigrants to Utah were Mormon converts in the 1870s. A large influx of Catholic Italians arrived after 1890 to work in the mines and for the railroad. St. Patrick's Church at 4th South and 10th West in Salt Lake City was built in 1914 and is the only surviving architectural evidence of their "Little Italy" community near the railroad tracks where many of them were employed. Their families have grown and they still have annual gatherings to celebrate their community, including Ferragosto in Salt Lake City.

"Greek town" was established on 2nd South between 4th and 6th West. The community started with a single Greek man in the 1870s and grew with the mining and railroads over the next several decades. Today, on the Holy Trinity Greek Orthodox Church they built in 1905 is the location of their annual "Greek Festival" in Salt Lake City, which welcomes all people in a celebration highlighted by fabulous Greek food and entertainment.

Nearby, "Little Syria" and "Lebanese town" were established near 3rd South and 5th West in SLC, providing a community for those folks who also worked on the railroads and in the mines. All evidence of this community is gone (except one restaurant in a different section of downtown) and most of the people of these communities have joined the mainstream population of Salt Lake City.

While the 1880 census shows Utah's increased foreign born population, it reflects not only the immigrants who came to find work in the mines and railroads, but also the increasing number of Mormon converts. The nations shown in this census include Africa (106), Asia (one), Australia (133), Austria (twenty-two), Belgium (five), Bohemia (three), Canada (1,036), Central America (one), China (502), Cuba (ninety-two), Denmark (7,791), England (19,654), France (129), Germany (885), Greece (two), Hawaii (thirty), Hungary (seven), India (seventeen), Ireland (1,321), Italy (138), Luxembourg (five), plus one from Malta. Some were born in Mexico (seventeen), Netherlands (141), Norway (1,214), Poland (sixteen), Portugal (four), Russia (fifty-four), Scotland (3,201), South America (twelve), Spain (seventy-six), Sweden (3,750), Switzerland (1,040), Turkey (eighty-six), Wales (2,390), the West Indies (seven), and twenty-three born at sea. There are those born in "Other Atlantic Islands" (forty), "Other Great Britain" (thirteen), "Other Pacific Islands" (seven), and "Other Europe" (twenty-two). The total foreign-born population was 43,994 out of a total population of 143,963.

The 1900 census shows a greater increase in foreign-born people, adding people from Finland (734), Japan (419), and Romania (one). The foreign-born total was 53,777 out of a total population of 276,749.

Japanese people arrived in Utah in 1890, with just five appearing in that census. They were mostly railroad as workers. "Japan town" was their neighborhood in Salt Lake City, although only their Buddhist temple and Christian Church remain today on 2nd South, between 2nd and 3rd West. While they did not get sent to "relocation camps" during WWII, they did work to become a part of the mainstream community and left "Japan town" behind after that war. Their annual Nihon Matsuri is a celebration of their culture, which welcomes all to that block of Salt Lake City.

Holy Trinity is the oldest Greek Orthodox church in Salt Lake City, but is no longer the only one. It was built in 1923. (*Author's collection*)

The lasting influence of these various groups of people in Utah is shown in the arrival of many other groups of people in Utah in the last 150 years since the arrival of the railroad. Some were immigrants, some refugees, and some sojourners who stayed for a short time before moving on to a more permanent home. Even today, Salt Lake City is ranked as twenty-fifth in refugee population in the United States.

These populations, while maintaining or reclaiming their individual identities, are "Like a quilt, the colors bleed together", enriching us all. The quote is from a colleague, Carol A. Jensen.

Ethnic Groups

This Church of Christ in "Japan Town" was built in 1924, reflecting the community in Salt Lake City. (*Author's collection*)

The newer Buddhist Temple is a reflection of a much older religious community in "Japan Town" in Salt Lake City. The first temple started in 1912. (*Author's collection*)

The shortage of iron and steel during World War II and the minimal use of the railroad tracks near Promontory Summit led to an event called "Undriven". The "Undriven" event at Promontory Summit in 1942 was part of a war effort to reclaim scrap metal for military use. The last spike was removed with great ceremony and the rails no longer in use from Corinne to Lucin were removed for use in the war effort. This photo is displayed by National Park Service at Golden Spike National Historic Site at Promontory Summit, Utah.

These engines are replicas of the original engines used at the Golden Spike Ceremony on May 10, 1869. They run three times a day from May 1 to mid-October with occasional maintenance days off noted on their website, along with the times for the demonstrations—great fun! (*Author's collection*)

APPENDIX

MUSEUMS AND WEBSITES

Bureau of Land Management Transcontinental Railroad Back Country Byway at www.blm.gov
California Emigrant Trail Interpretive Center, Elko, Nevada at www.californiatrailcenter.org and at HWY I-80, Exit 292, 8 miles West of Elko, NV
Corinne Hell on Wheels display at the gas station in Corinne
Fort Douglas Military Museum, 32 Potter St, Salt Lake City, UT
Golden Spike National Historic Site at Promontory Summit, UT
Library of Congress at www.loc.gov
National Records and Archives Administration at www.archives.gov
Ogden Station, Ogden, UT
Railroad Museum at Ogden Station, Ogden, UT
Richmond Museum, Richmond, CA
Stewart Library Weber State University, Ogden, UT
Utah State Archives, 300 South Rio Grande St., Salt Lake City, UT
Utah State Historical Society, 300 South Rio Grande St., Salt Lake City, UT

BIBLIOGRAPHY

Alexander, Thomas G. *Utah, The Right Place*. Gibbs Smith, 2003.
Brooks, Juanita. *History of the Jews in Utah and Idaho*. Western Epics, Salt Lake City, UT, 1973
Bullinger's Postal and Shippers Guide for the United States and Canada, 1922
Bureau of Land Management. Rails East to Promontory: The Utah Stations, www.nps.gov/parkhistory/online_books/blm/ut/8/bibliography.htm
Cheu, Richard. "The Chinese Transcontinental Railroad Workers" 2018 Golden Spike Conference. Marriott Downtown, Salt Lake City, UT. May 12, 2018.
Chinese Railroad Workers in North America Project at Stanford University. "Chinese Workers and the Railroad". web.stanford.edu/group/chineserailroad/cgi-bin/wordpress/.
Daughters of Utah Pioneers. International Society Daughters of Utah Pioneers, 2018.
Deitch, JoAnne Weisman, ed. *A Century of Westward Expansion: Researching American History*. Discovery Enterprises, Ltd., Carlisle, MA, 2000
Dodge , G.M. 1868Map of the Union Pacific Rail Road and surveys of 1864, 65, 66, 67, 1868 from Missouri River to Humboldt Wells, _ Library of Congress
Doolittle, John T. Congressional Record Online via GPO Access [wais.access.gpo.gov], April 29, 1999 at cprr.org/Museum/Chinese.html.
Hampshire, David, Martha Sonntag Bradley and Allen Roberts. *A History of Summit County*. Utah State Historical Society, 1998
Hart, Alfred A. and Andrew J. Andrew J. Russell. "Train of Iron". Union Pacific Museum in Omaha, Nebraska. 2018.
Huchel, Frederick M. *A History of Box Elder County*, Utah State Historical Society, 1999
Jordan, Donald and Timothy J. O'Keefe, eds. *The Irish in the San Francisco Bay Area*. Irish Literary and Historical Society, 2005.
Kelen, Leslie G. and Sandra T. Fuller. *The Other Utahns: A Photographic Portfolio*. University of Utah Press, 1988.
Kreck, Dick. *Hell on Wheels: Wicked Towns Along the Union Pacific Railroad*. Fulcrum Publishing, 2013.
Mann, David H. "The Undriving of the Golden Spike", *Utah Historical Quarterly*, Vol. 37, No. 1, Winter 1969.
McCormick, S. and John R. Sillito. *A World We Thought We Knew: readings in Utah History*. University of Utah Press, 1995.

Bibliography

Merritt, Chris and Eric Cheng. Historical Review of Chinese Railroad Workers' Contribution. 2018 Golden Spike Conference. Marriott Downtown, Salt Lake City, UT. May 11, 2018.
National Archives and Records Administration. Major United States Laws Relating to Immigration and Naturalization: 1790–2005. November 2014.
www.archives.gov/files/research/naturalization/420-major-immigration-laws.pdf.
National Park Service. Golden Spike NHS: Cultural Landscape Report. http://npshistory.com/series/archeology/mr/16/clr2.htm
National Park Service. The Joining of a Nation. May 18, 2018 . www.nps.gov/gosp/index.htm.
National Park Service. Long Distance Communication. June 8, 2018. https://www.nps.gov/poex/index.htm.
National Society of the Sons of Utah Pioneers. National Society of the Sons of Utah Pioneers. 2018. https://www.sup1847.com/.
Papanikolas, Helen Z., ed. *The Peoples of Utah*, Utah State Historical Society, 1976.
Poll, Richard D., Thomas G. Alexander, Eugene E. Campbell, and David E. Miller. *Utah's History*. Brigham Young University Press, Provo, UT, 1978
Powell, Allan Kent, ed.. *Utah History Encyclopedia*. University of Utah Press, 1994.
Rand, McNally and Company. 1883Map exhibiting the several Pacific railroads _ Library of Congress
Rand, McNally and Company. 1900The Union Pacific system of railroad and steamship lines, 1900. _ Library of Congress
Raymond, Anan. *The Promontory Branch of the First Continental Railroad in Utah 1869–1904*, Bureau of Land Management
Roberts, Richard C. and Richard W. Sadler. *A History of Weber County*. Utah State Historical Society, 1997.
Roberts, Richard C. and Richard W. Sadler. *Ogden: Junction City*. Windsor Publications, 1985.
Sillito, John and Sarah Langsdon. *Images of America: Ogden*. Arcadia Press, 2008
Sillito, Linda. *A History of Salt Lake County*. Utah State Historical Society, 1996.
Stone, Eileen Hallet. *Historic Tales of Utah*. History Press, 2016.
Stone, Eileen Hallet. *A Homeland in the West: Utah Jews Remember*. University of Utah Press, Salt Lake City, UT, 2001
Utah State Gazetteer and Business Directory, 1903–1904, Volume 2
Wolfe, Linda Gunter. *Travel By Rail*. Bear Wallow Books, Publishers, Inc., Indianapolis, IN 2015
Yang, John H., comp. *Asian Americans in Utah: A Living History*. State of Utah Office of Asian Affairs, 1999.

ACKNOWLEDGMENTS

Chinese Railroad Workers Descendants Association for support and inspiration
Carol A. Jensen (colleague and source of great encouragement)
Chris Saffell (travel buddy and colleague)
Eric Yuanchin Cheng (Chief Railroad Engineer of the Utah Department of Transportation) for his encouragement
Jinger Bennett LaGuardia (friend and motivator)
Judge Michael Kwan for his encouragement
Kate and John Saffell (website, data entry, photos)
Lisa Yang (film maker) for her encouragement
Margaret Yee (Sister Cities colleague) for her encouragement
Richard Cheu for his assistance and encouragement
Sarah Singh (Special Collections, Weber State University, Ogden, UT)

INDEX

10-mile marker 58

Africa 19, 23, 83, 87
Auerbach 15-16
Australia 19, 83, 87
Austria 19, 83, 87

Balfour 37
Baptist 77, 79, 81, 87
Bear River 25, 37, 39
Belgium 83, 87
Bidwell–Bartleson 9–10
Blue Creek 37, 41
Bohemia 83, 87
Bonneville 37
Bovine 50
Box Elder 14, 92
Brigham City 7, 13-14, 37-38
British Isles 13
Brooks 15, 92
Buddhist 87, 89

California 10, 13, 15, 19, 41, 85, 91
Camp Floyd 15
Camp Victory **58**-59
Canada 37, 83, 87, 92
Carthage 13
Castle Rock 30-31
Catholic 19, 77, 79, 86, 87
Centre 58
China/Chinese 19, 41, 44-45, 48-49, 70, 72, 75, 83-87, 92-93, 95

Congregational 77, 82
Connor 19-20, 37
Corinne 15-17, 37, 39-40, 52, 73, 77, 79-82, 90-91
Cornish 13
Croydon 30, 33
Cuba 87

Dale Creek 24
Danish/Denmark 13-14, 83, 87
Devil's Gate 30

Echo 7, 11, 23, 28, 30, 32
Elinor 57
Emory 30-31
England/English 19, 23, 81, 83, 87
Episcopal 77-79, 81

Finland/Finn 13, 87
Fort Buenaventura 9, 30
Fort Douglas 19-20, 91
France 19, 83, 87

German 13, 15, 19, 23, 83, 87
Golden Spike 7, 15, 22, 41-42, 58-61, 63, 71, 76-77, 79, 83, 90-93
Gravel Pit 50
Great Salt Lake 9-10, 52
Greece/Greek 83, 87-88
Green River 25

Hanging Rock 30

Hart 41, 47-48, 59-67, 92
Hawaii 14, 83, 87
Hollander 14
Humboldt Wells 9-10, 92
Hungarian/Hungary 15, 83, 87

India 9, 19, 30, 87, 94
Iosepa 14
Ireland/Irish 13, 19, 23, 41, 75, 83, 86-87, 92
Italian/Italy 19, 83, 86-87

Japan 85, 87-89
Jewish 15, 19

Kelton 55-57
Kosmo 57-58

Lake 9-10, 13-15, 19-20, 52, 57-58, 73, 77-78, 81, 83-84, 86-89, 91-94
Lampo 37
Lebanese 87
Lucin 49-52, 58, 90
Lutheran 81
Luxembourg 87

Malta 87
Manti 13
Matlin 50
Medea 50
Metatarus 58
Methodist 77, 79, 81-82
Mexican/Mexico 9, 13, 19, 83, 87
Monument 20, 57
Morgan 30, 33
Mount Pleasant 13

Nella 57
Netherland 19, 83, 87
Norway 19, 83, 87

Ogden 9-10, 14-15, 18-20, 27, 30, 35-36, 71, 73, 76-78, 81-83, 86, 91, 94-95
Ombey 55-56
Peplin 55
Peterson 30, 34

Poland 19, 83, 87
Pony Express 11, 21, 31
Portugal 19, 83, 87
Presbyterian 77, 79-81
Promontory Summit 7, 15, 23, 28, 37, 41-42, 49, 58-62, 68, 70-71, 75-76, 79, 83, 90-93

Red Dome 50
Romania 87
Romola 50
Rozel 58-59
Russell 23, 27, 39, 42, 58, 65, 68-70, 92
Russia 15, 83, 87

Salt Lake City 13-15, 19-20, 73, 77-78, 81, 83-84, 86-89, 91-94
Scandinavian 13
Scotland 19, 83, 87
Seco 57
Spain/Spanish 9, 19, 83, 87
Stokes 37
Strawberry 30
Surbon 37
Sweden 13, 81, 83, 87
Swiss/Switzerland 14, 19, 83, 87
Syria 87

Ten-Mile 57, 59-60
Terrace 50, 53-55
Turkey 87

Uintah 30, 34
Umbria 50

Wahsatch 23, 29
Walden 50
Wales 19, 83, 87
Watercress 50, 52-55
Weber 7, 12, 23, 30, 33, 36, 91, 94-95
Welsh 13
West Indies 83, 87
Willard 37-38

Zias 55